A Note to Parents

Dorling Kindersley Readers is a compelling new program for beginning readers, designed in conjunction with leading literacy experts, including Dr. Linda Gambrell, President of the National Reading Conference and past board member of the International Reading Association.

Beautiful illustrations and superb full-color photographs combine with engaging, easy-to-read stories to offer a fresh approach to each subject in the series. Each *Dorling Kindersley Reader* is guaranteed to capture a child's interest while developing his or her reading skills, general knowledge, and love of reading.

The four levels of *Dorling Kindersley Readers* are aimed at different reading abilities, enabling you to choose the books that are exactly right for your child:

Level 1 – Beginning to read
Level 2 – Beginning to read alone
Level 3 – Reading alone
Level 4 – Proficient readers

The "normal" age at which a child begins to read can be anywhere from three to eight years old, so these levels are intended only as a general guideline.

No matter which level you select, you can be sure that you are helping your child learn to read, then read to learn!

A DK PUBLISHING BOOK

www.dk.com

Created by Leapfrog Press Ltd.

Project Editor Naia Bray-Moffatt
Art Editor Jane Horne

For DK Publishing
Senior Editor Linda Esposito
Senior Art Editor Diane Thistlethwaite
U.S. Editor Regina Kahney
Production Josie Alabaster
Picture Researcher Liz Moore
Photographer Andy Crawford
Ballet Consultant Alison Good

Reading Consultant
Linda B. Gambrell, Ph.D.

First American Edition, 1999
4 6 8 10 9 7 5 3
Published in the United States by DK Publishing, Inc.
95 Madison Avenue, New York, New York 10016

Published in Great Britain by Dorling Kindersley Limited.

Library of Congress Cataloging-in-Publication Data
Grindley, Sally.
The little ballerina / by Sally Grindley. -- 1st American ed.
p. cm. -- (Dorling Kindersley readers. Level 2)
Summary: Follows the activities of a group of young students in their ballet class.
ISBN 0-7894-4005-9 (hard). ISBN 0-7894-4004-0 (pbk.)
1. Ballet--Juvenile literature. 2. Ballet dancing--Juvenile literature.
[1. Ballet.] I. Title. II. Series.
GV1787.5.G75 1999
792.8--dc21
99-11610
CIP

Color reproduction by Colourscan, Singapore
Printed and bound in China by L Rex

The publisher would like to thank the following for their kind permission to reproduce their photographs:
Key: t=top, a=above, b=below, l=left, r=right, c=center

Camera Press: 9br; /**Andrew Crickmay**: 31tr; **Mary Evans Picture Library**: 5br; **Royal Opera House/Catherine Ashmore:** 25tr Models: Amy Berry, Naia Bray-Moffatt, Rosie Fisher, Alison Good, Robyn Hewitt, Alex Johns, Lizzie Knight, Siobhan McCleod, Guy and Jack Westbrook, and Olivia and Grace Williams.

In addition, Dorling Kindersley would like to thank: Avril Mills for permission to photograph in her ballet studio, Dance-A-Ramix.
Gill Cossey and Monica Clark of Chameleons Face Painting, Woking.

The Little Ballerina

Written by Sally Grindley

DK
DK PUBLISHING, INC.

Laura pulled on her leotard
in front of her bedroom mirror.
She bent her legs
and then stood again.
It was a perfect plié (plee-AY).

“Hurry up!”
said Laura’s mother.
“You don’t want
to be late for
ballet school today.”

French names

Ballet steps have French names because they were first written down in France more than 300 years ago. French king Louis XIV (1638–1715) danced in several ballets.

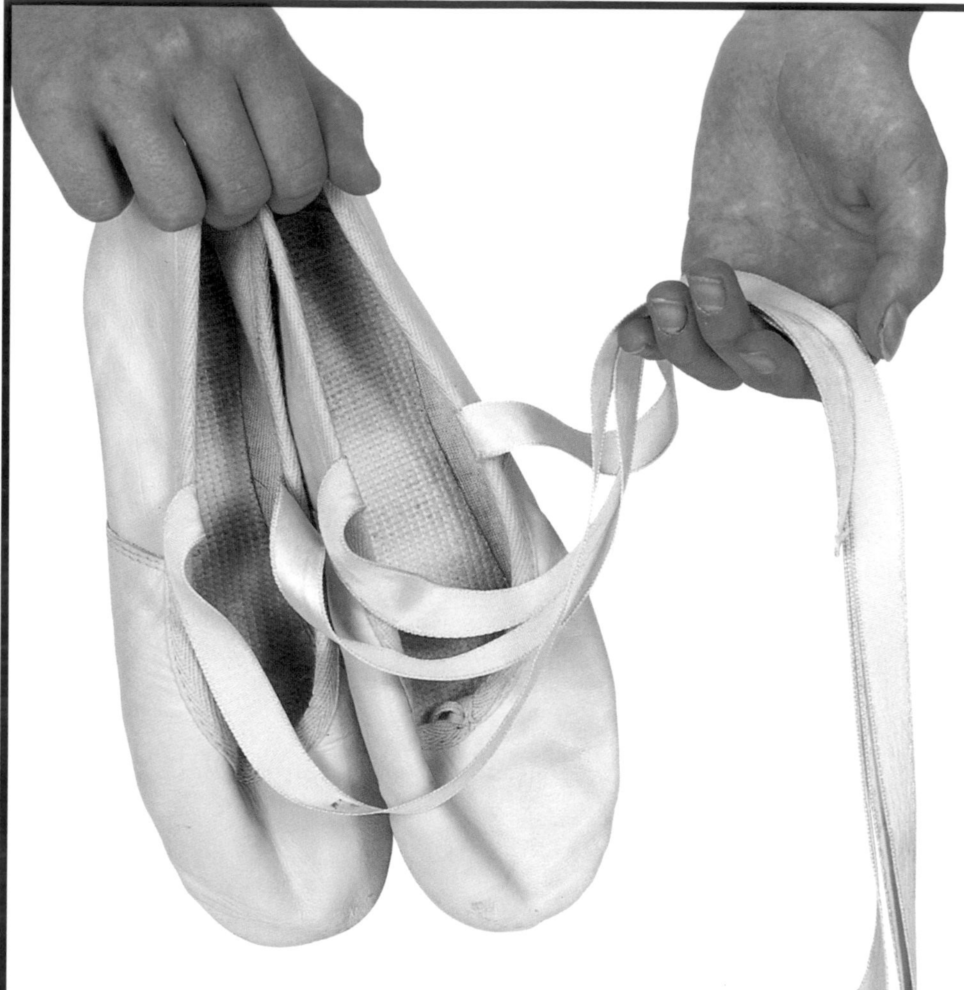

Laura opened a closet and
took out her best ballet shoes.
Today the school
was putting on a show –
The Big Bad Dog and the
Two Little Kittens.

Ballet shoes
For practicing, ballet dancers wear leather or canvas shoes held on with ribbons or elastic. Satin shoes are usually worn only for shows.

Laura had a part as a rabbit. She couldn't wait to dance in her first show.

"Good luck," said Laura's mom on the way to school.

At the school, Laura looked for her best friend, Miranda.
But she didn't see Miranda anywhere.
The other children chatted happily as they put on their shoes.

"In you come,"
said their teacher, Mrs. Beth.
"Straight to the barre and warm up."
Laura stood at the wooden rail.
"Where's Miranda?" she said
to herself.

Using the barre
Dancers hold on to the barre, the wooden rail, to keep steady while they practice.

"Hold on to the barre,"
said Mrs. Beth.
"Feet in first position.
And gentle pliés
in time to the music."

Laura knew all five positions by heart:

In first position,
your heels touch and
your toes turn out
to the side.

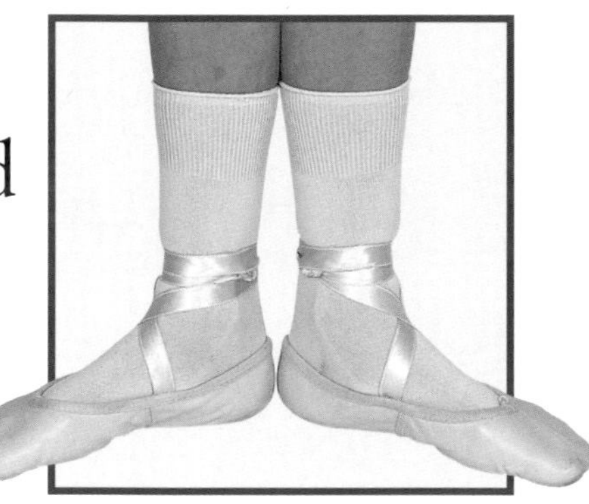

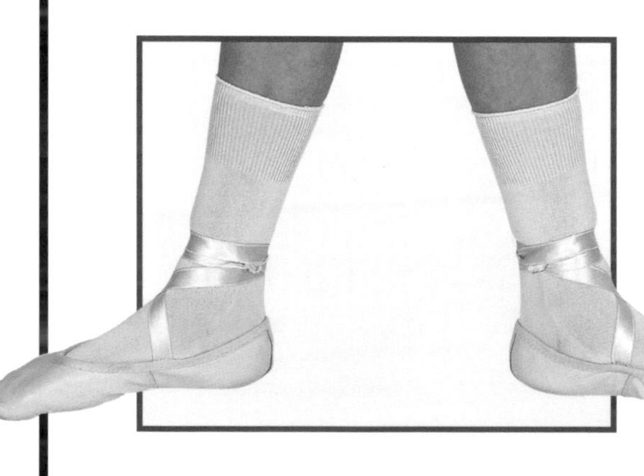

In second position,
your feet
are apart.

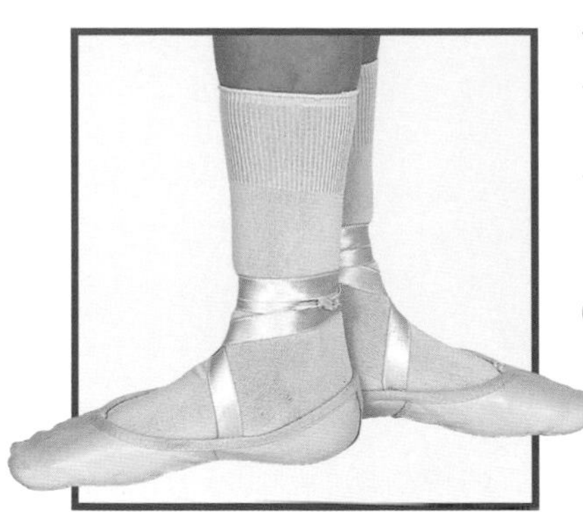

In third position,
the heel of one foot
goes halfway in front
of the other foot.

In fourth position,
the right foot goes
in front of the left,
a foot's length
between them.

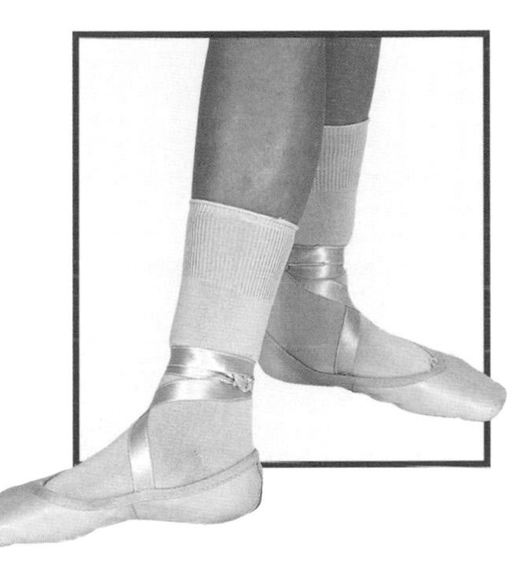

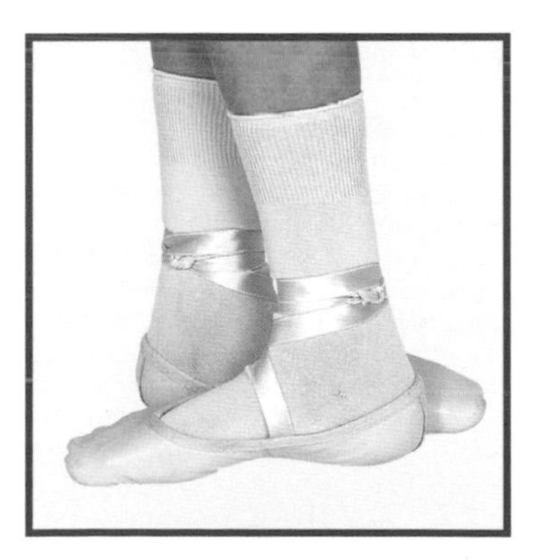

In fifth position,
your front foot is
placed flat against
your back foot.

Laura tried hard
as she did her
steps at the barre.

Then the class
did arm movements.

"Let your head and eyes
follow the movements
of your arms,"
called out Mrs. Beth.
Laura moved
her hands
lightly around
her body.

"We'll stop there,"
called out Mrs. Beth.
"Come and sit down."

Laura sat on the floor
with the other dancers.
"Poor Miranda
has hurt her foot.
She won't be able
to dance today."

The children gasped.
Miranda was one of the kittens.

Who would play her part?

"I'd like you to take her place, Laura.
You practiced all the steps
with Miranda."
Laura felt excited and scared.
She had one of the main parts
in the ballet now!

Laura's hands shook
as she put on Miranda's cat suit.
"Meow," said Kate, the other kitten.
"Meow," Laura giggled,
and felt a little better.

Just then Jane, the Big Bad Dog,
danced in on tiptoe.
Angie, the Good Witch, joined her.
"Hooray!" everyone cheered.
Jane and Angie were the best dancers
in the school.

While the other children put on their costumes, Laura practiced with Kate, Jane, and Angie.

Dancing on pointe
Older dancers with strong legs and feet wear pointe shoes. With pointe shoes they can dance on the tips of their toes.

At the end of the ballet
Laura had to do an arabesque
(ar-uh-BESK).
"Try one now," said Mrs. Beth.
Laura stood on one leg
with the other leg
stretched out behind.
Suddenly her ankle wobbled.

"You can do it," said Mrs. Beth.
"Stare at something
straight in front of you."
Laura stared at the clock
and lifted her leg again.
This time she didn't wobble.

"Makeup time!" called Mrs. Beth. She painted Kate and Laura's faces to look like kittens.

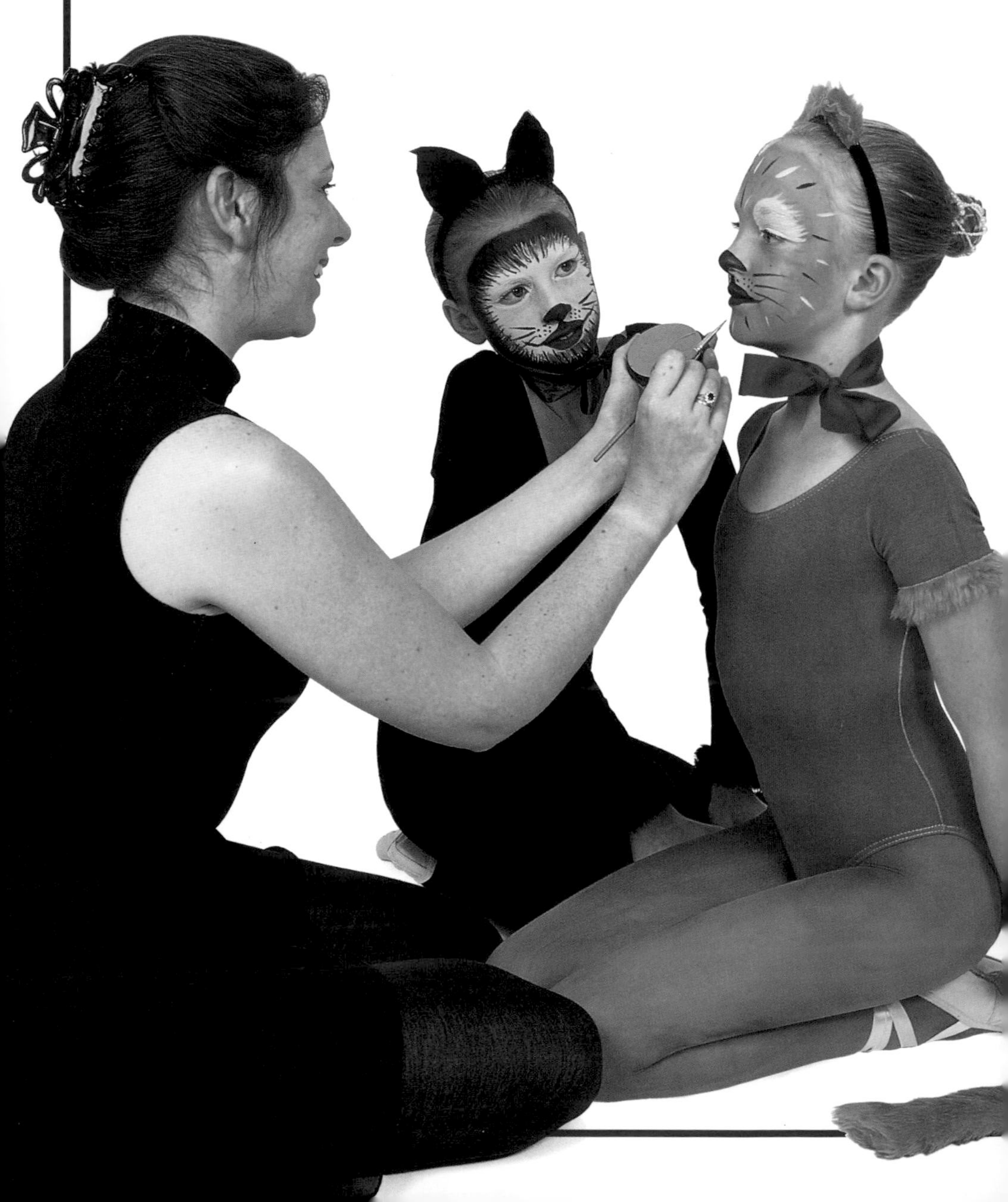

Then she checked everyone's
costumes and makeup.
"We're ready!" said Mrs. Beth.
"Walk to the hall
and wait behind the stage.
Good luck, everyone."

Laura stood in the wings
at the side of the stage.
Then the ballet began.

The Big Bad Dog
leaped across the stage
in a grand jeté (gron she-TAY).

The stage
Names are given to different parts of a stage. The wings are at either side of the stage.

Behind her came the Good Witch and the rest of Laura's class.

Then it was Laura's turn
to go on stage.
Her heart beat faster.
"Pas de chat," (pah de SHAH)
Laura said to herself
as she and Kate jumped sideways
across the stage like cats.

In the front row
Laura's mother looked surprised.
Laura was supposed
to be a rabbit!

Laura danced the steps
she had practiced.
The music helped her and
she began to feel like a kitten.
She forgot all about the audience.

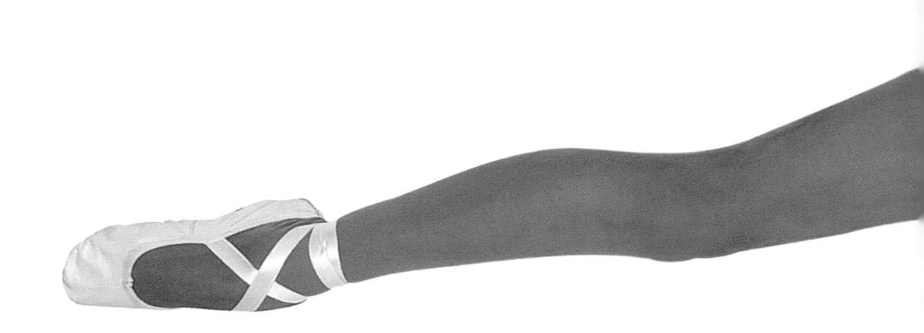

Then it was time
for the arabesque.
Laura stood on one leg
and raised the other.

She felt her ankle wobble.
Then she saw a clock
in the wings.
She stared hard at it –
and balanced perfectly!

As the ballet ended
the audience began to clap.
Laura and the other dancers
took their bows.
Laura smiled at her mother,
who was clapping wildly.

Bow
Dancers bow to their teacher at the end of a class, or to the audience at the end of a show.

Laura thought being a ballet dancer was the best thing in the world!

Some ballet steps

Plié (plee-AY)
Movement in which the knees bend.

Battement-tendus
(bat-MON ton-DOO)
Exercise in which the foot is slid along the floor until it points.

Grand jeté
(gron she-TAY)
A big jump from one leg to the other, with legs outstretched in the air.

Pas de chat
(pah de SHAH)
"Step of the cat":
a leap sideways.

Pirouette (peer-uh-WET)
A dancer spins around on one leg.

Arabesque (ar-uh-BESK)
A dancer stands on one leg and lifts the other straight up behind.